# COUNTRY INSIGHTS
# DENMARK

Ole Steen Hansen

RSVP
RAINTREE
Steck-Vaughn
PUBLISHERS
The Steck-Vaughn Company

*Austin, Texas*

# COUNTRY INSIGHTS

## BRAZIL • CHINA • CUBA • CZECH REPUBLIC • DENMARK • FRANCE
## INDIA • JAMAICA • JAPAN • KENYA • MEXICO • PAKISTAN

---

### GUIDE TO THIS BOOK

**Besides telling you about the whole of Denmark, this book looks closely at the city of Århus and the village of Hyllested.**

**This city symbol will appear at the top of the page and information boxes each time the book discusses Århus.**

**This rural symbol will appear each time the book discusses Hyllested.**

---

**Title Page:** Girls rowing a boat on a lake in one of Denmark's popular parks, on Bornholm Island

**Contents page:** Playing ice hockey on a frozen lake in Grenå.

Published by Raintree Steck-Vaughn Publishers, an imprint of Steck-Vaughn Company

**Library of Congress Cataloging-in-Publication Data**
Hansen, Ole Steen.
Denmark / Ole Steen Hansen.
    p.   cm.—(Country Insights)
Includes bibliographical references and index.
Summary: Introduces the geography, economics, and social structure of the smallest and most southern country of Scandinavia.
ISBN 0-8172-4794-7
1. Denmark—Juvenile literature.
I. Title.  II. Series.
[1. Denmark.]
DL109.H36   1998
948.9—dc21          97-11622

Printed in Italy. Bound in the United States.
1 2 3 4 5 6 7 8 9 0 02 01 00 99 98

# Contents

# Introducing Denmark

Denmark is the smallest and most southerly of the countries of Scandinavia, which lie in northern Europe. It is probably best known for the fairy tales of Hans Christian Andersen and for being home to powerful Viking raiders a thousand years ago. Denmark's own story is of a small country, with limited natural resources, that has become one of the five richest countries in the world today.

A thousand years ago, Danish Vikings conquered and controlled large areas of northern Europe. But since then, Denmark has lost many wars and has been occupied by other nations several times. Today, it is one of the smallest countries in Europe, with a population smaller than London's. Its capital city is Copenhagen.

Denmark has its own distinctive traditions and a tongue-twisting language that includes several different dialects. It is a very independent country. Although Denmark is a member of the European Union (EU), recently it has been reluctant to work more closely with the EU and give up some of its independence.

*The city of Copenhagen, the capital of Denmark. Copenhagen has few very high buildings. The large building with a light-green roof is the national parliament.*

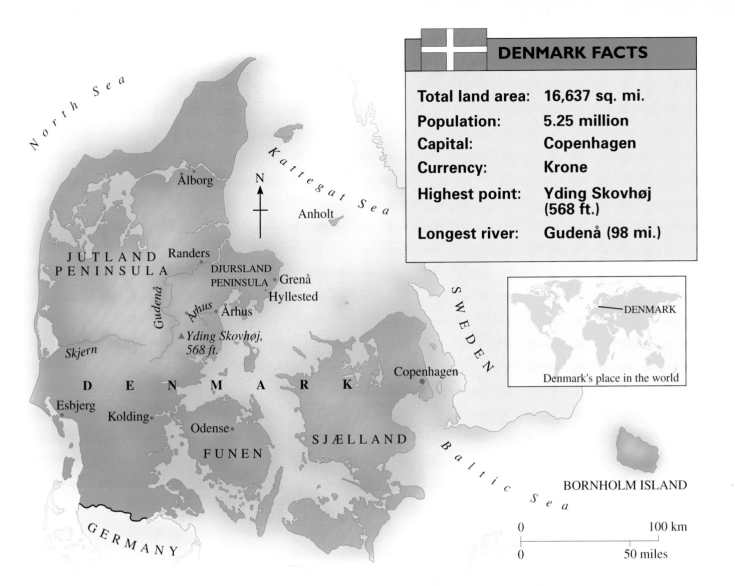

**DENMARK FACTS**

| | |
|---|---|
| Total land area: | 16,637 sq. mi. |
| Population: | 5.25 million |
| Capital: | Copenhagen |
| Currency: | Krone |
| Highest point: | Yding Skovhøj (568 ft.) |
| Longest river: | Gudenå (98 mi.) |

DENMARK

Denmark's place in the world

North Sea

Kattegat Sea

N

Ålborg

Anholt

JUTLAND PENINSULA

Randers

DJURSLAND PENINSULA

Grenå

Hyllested

Gudenå

Århus

Århus

Yding Skovhøj, 568 ft.

Skjern

SWEDEN

D E N M A R K

Esbjerg

Kolding

Odense

FUNEN

SJÆLLAND

Copenhagen

Baltic Sea

BORNHOLM ISLAND

GERMANY

0          100 km

0          50 miles

Wealth in Denmark is shared more evenly than in most other countries, because people pay high taxes. Many workers pay more than 50 percent of their wages in taxes. The money is used to pay for a welfare system that includes health care, benefits for the unemployed and the elderly, and public services. Compared with the rest of the world, it is difficult to become either very rich or very poor in Denmark.

▼ *Queen Margrethe II of Denmark on a visit to a seaside town. Denmark is the oldest monarchy in Europe.*

# THE CITY OF ÅRHUS

Århus (pronounced "Or´hoose") is the second-largest city in Denmark after Copenhagen. The city first grew around the mouth of the Århus River, around A.D. 900, during the Viking Age. The sheltered natural harbor made the site an ideal place for trade.

### ÅRHUS'S NAME

The name "Århus" comes from an early Danish word meaning "river mouth." In Danish, the letter "Å" means a small river or a large stream. The city was named after its position at the mouth of the Århus River.

In the nineteenth century, manufacturing industries developed in the city and provided work for many people. At the same time, a network of railroads was built across Denmark, and Århus became an important railroad center.

*Restaurants and cafés along the banks of the Århus River*

During World War II (1939–1945), the German army occupied the city. After the war, one of the military airbases they had built was turned into the city airport.

▼ **Good national and international transportation links are still very important to Århus. This train has just arrived from Hamburg, in Germany.**

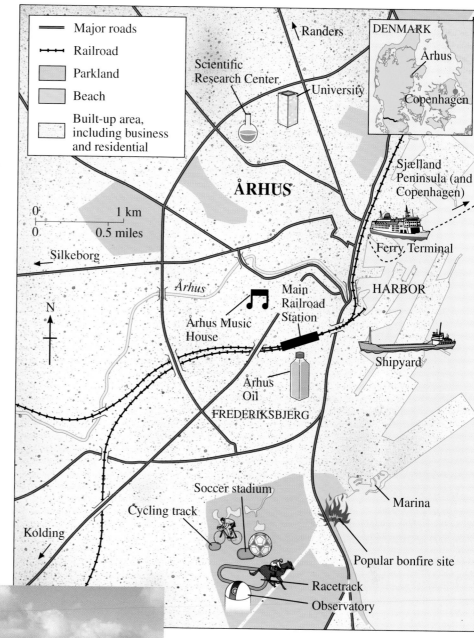

| | |
|---|---|
| —— | Major roads |
| +++ | Railroad |
| | Parkland |
| | Beach |
| | Built-up area, including business and residential |

Randers

Scientific Research Center

University

DENMARK

Århus

Copenhagen

ÅRHUS

Sjælland Peninsula (and Copenhagen)

0    1 km
0    0.5 miles

Silkeborg

Ferry Terminal

Århus

HARBOR

N

Århus Music House

Main Railroad Station

Shipyard

Århus Oil

FREDERIKSBJERG

Kolding

Soccer stadium

Cycling track

Marina

Popular bonfire site

Racetrack

Observatory

By the 1930s, Århus had become a university town. Today it is one of the most important educational centers in Denmark, which helps to make Århus very attractive to young people. Many come from distant parts of Denmark to live and study in the city.

# THE VILLAGE OF HYLLESTED

*The landscape around Hyllested is typically Danish,*
*with cultivated farmland surrounding the village.*

Hyllested (pronounced "Hool-a-stur") is a small village set in beautiful countryside on the Djursland peninsula. The village is considered to be in a remote location by Danish standards, although Denmark is not really big enough for anywhere to be remote.

Sixty years ago, most people in Hyllested were employed in farming or in the gravel pits near the village. Many worked in the fields of the nearby Rugård Farm. Most people rode the two miles to the fields of Rugård on a bicycle.

## HYLLESTED'S NAME

Hyllested's name can be traced back to the year 1183, when the village was known as *Hildir´s sted,* meaning Hildir´s place. Hildir was a Viking man's name.

The railroad line that ran through the village made Hyllested a local center for neighboring farms and villages. There were stores, crafts, and a mill. People could buy most of their daily needs in Hyllested, including clothes, shoes, and all kinds of local foods. To children from neighboring farms, Hyllested was "the big town," where they went to take their farms' crops to the mill.

Today, only the houses are left in Hyllested—the railroad line, the mill, and every single store are gone, as people have moved from the countryside to the cities. Rugård Farm is still a working farm, but most of the work is done using machinery rather than by hand, which means fewer people are needed. Many young people leave the village to search for jobs or to go to colleges in the cities.

*Hyllested village church. White churches are a typical feature of Danish villages. The oldest parts of this church are 800 years old.*

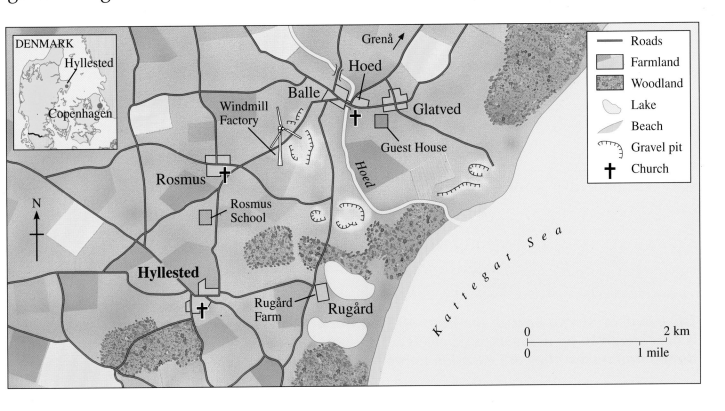

# Land and Climate

Denmark is a country of few extremes. Its landscape is made up of gently rolling hills, cultivated fields, and a well-kept countryside. There are few wild, uncultivated areas, no volcanoes or earthquakes, few poisonous animals, and the landscape is one of the flattest in the world.

Denmark consists of a mainland peninsula—the Jutland Peninsula—and 406 small and large islands, 325 of which are uninhabited. The many islands give Denmark a total coastline of 4,545 miles.

The climate is influenced by Denmark's position between the North Sea and the Baltic Sea. Since there is no place in the country that is more than 50 miles from the sea, there are few variations in climate between different places. Denmark is as far north as central Canada, but it seldom gets the same icy winters, although there are usually snowy days every year. In the summer, the sea is slow to warm, which means summer days are often quite cool.

*The island of Strynø Kalv, in the front of the photograph, is considered to be uninhabited, because, although it has three farmhouses, they are vacation homes.*

The most extreme form of Denmark's climate is its violent winds. In the winter, occasional snowstorms can block roads and prevent people from going to school or to work. When storms happen at the same time as high tides, there are sometimes floods. But such extremes are rare. Usually, Danish children just hope for colder days and more snow in the winter and warmer weather for a trip to the beach in the summer.

▲ *This old tree was blown down by a storm in the early spring.*

◄ *Ice-skating on the lakes of Copenhagen. Some winters are so cold that the lakes and even the sea around the coast freeze.*

## DENMARK'S CLIMATE

| | |
|---|---|
| Average daily temperature: | January: 32° F |
| | July: 60° F |
| Highest recorded temperature: | 96.8° F (1975) |
| Lowest recorded temperature: | −25.6° F (1982) |

# SHAPED BY ICE

The landscape around Århus was formed during the Ice Age, around 15,000 years ago. The city is surrounded by hills made of clay and gravel that were pushed up by the huge glacier that once covered Denmark. The path of the Århus River was also carved out at this time by streams of water running from the glacier.

Today Århus stretches out along a bay. Although the city is quite big, open country is not far from its outskirts, and there are several small forests nearby.

▼ *Autumn colors in the forests of the wildlife park, just south of Århus*

People who live in Århus can combine the benefits of city life with easy access to woods, beaches, and the countryside.

City life changes greatly with the weather. Winters are often wet and gray. But when the snow comes, children in Århus make the most of it by skiing, sledding, and having snowball fights in the city hills. Spring's warmer weather is always welcomed, and it brings people out in large numbers around the city squares and street cafés.

*The hills around* ▶
*Århus are ideal*
*for sledding—on*
*toboggans, trays,*
*or anything else*
*that can be found.*

Since Denmark is so far north, there are longer summer days and lighter nights than in countries farther south. It is traditional to celebrate the lightest summer nights by singing midsummer songs around huge bonfires. In Århus, a popular place for this is the beach just south of the marina, in Århus Harbor.

▼ *A summer bonfire on the beach shortly after 10:00 P.M. The sun has just set, but there will be a soft light on the northern horizon throughout the night.*

# LIFE THROUGH FOUR SEASONS

Hyllested, like Århus, is also surrounded by hills formed during the Ice Age. The landscape is also made up of large deposits of stones and gravel. The area has a long tradition of gravel extraction from these deposits, where gravel is taken from pits and sold. The work used to be done by hand, but it is now done mostly by machinery. The gravel is used in road construction all over Djursland and farther west in Jutland.

Farmers in Hyllested are affected much more by the changing seasons than city people are, since the success of their crops is dependent on the weather conditions. Spring and early summer, from March to May, should bring a fair amount of rain. This is the growing season in Denmark.

**▼ Gravel extraction in a pit just outside Hyllested**

**This ripe crop has ▶ been flattened by a thunderstorm. Bad thunderstorms can reduce the value of a harvest by 50 percent.**

Late summer should be warm and sunny, and this helps the crops dry out before the harvest. But since the Danish weather is always changing, it is rarely as everyone would like it to be.

In winter snowstorms, Hyllested is occasionally cut off by snowdrifts, which block the roads leading to the village and make it impossible to drive cars through. The smaller roads leading to the village are always the last to be cleared when there is heavy snow, since the bigger, main roads, which are used by more traffic, have to be cleared first. If the village is cut off and someone is dangerously ill or just about to have a baby the rescue services use armored personnel carriers from the army to reach Hyllested and get them to the hospital.

▲ *An armored personnel carrier sets out to rescue sick people in Hyllested who are snowed in. The weather may not look bad in town, but in the countryside, snowdrifts quickly cut off farms and villages.*

15

# Home Life

There have been great changes in family life in Denmark. Thirty-five years ago, most people lived in a household of at least three people. Today, 46 percent of the population live either alone or in households of just two.

The high standard of living means that several generations seldom live under the same roof, as they do in poorer countries. When elderly people can no longer cope with living on their own, they usually move to old people's homes or to housing built specially for them. Most young people leave home at an early age and get their own places. Many wait until their late twenties before they marry, to finish their education. They live with friends before settling down to raise a family. In many towns, apartments have been built specially for young people.

◀ *A typical Danish house being built with traditional red bricks, and (above) the finished house. Most people in Denmark live in single-family houses.*

## FAVORITE DANISH DISHES

Pastas, pizzas, and hamburgers have become very popular with young Danes recently. But some traditional Danish dishes continue to be popular, too. Roast pork with brown gravy, boiled potatoes, and carrots has long been considered the national dish. Meatballs with potato salad is another favorite, especially eaten out of doors. For lunch, most people eat open sandwiches of black bread with different meats, cheese, or salad.

*Arguments such as "Who'll wash the dishes?" have been replaced by "Who'll load the dishwasher?" —one-third of all Danish families owns a dishwasher.*

Another reason for the rising number of small households is the growing number of divorces. It is expected that at the turn of the twentieth century, a third of all Danish children will have experienced divorce in their family.

Most Danish homes are well equipped with goods such as televisions, video recorders, and washing machines. Many also have spin driers and dishwashers. Computers have become very popular recently, and soon more than half of all Danish households will own at least one.

# AT HOME IN ÅRHUS

Since 30,000 young people study in Århus, there is always a shortage of smaller homes for people living on their own. For many students, "home" is a small, overpriced room. Camilla is an eighteen-year-old student in Århus who grew up in a fishing village and left home when she was sixteen. She is lucky to have found a reasonable-sized place to live, with a large bedroom. She shares a bathroom and a kitchen with another girl in a similar room. Their rooms are in a modern, semidetached house with a small yard. The only disadvantage is that it is quite far from the city center.

"I love my home because I like making my own decisions, like tidying and cleaning up. I like visiting my parents in the village, but prefer to live on my own."—Camilla Hjortshøj, 18 years old, student

*Her home may not be a castle, but Camilla likes having her own place.*

Students and old people in Århus tend to live close to the center of the city, whereas most families with children live in modern apartments or houses in the fast-spreading suburbs. In the western parts of the city, there are tall apartment buildings, where many refugees and immigrants have settled in recent years.

Closer to the city center is an area with many small apartments, called Frederiksbjerg. The apartments were built about 100 years ago for workers and their families. Today most of the apartments are home to either students or the elderly. Some have shared toilets and a bath in the basement.

▲ The Frederiksbjerg area, with typical Danish four- and five-story houses

◀ A Vietnamese immigrant buying vegetables in an Århus market

# HOME LIFE IN HYLLESTED

Hyllested today is in some ways like a suburb in a big city. People have their homes there, but they shop and work in other places. Villagers can buy groceries and essentials in the villages of Balle or Tirstrup, a few miles away, but if they want anything more specialized, they have to drive to the larger towns of Grenå or Ebeltoft, over 9 miles away.

Peter Vinther and Dorte Fleischer have a typical modern village family. They both grew up in Hyllested, and they liked it so much they decided to raise their own family there. Their house, like all the houses in the village, has a yard where they can keep rabbits and play with their dog. Peter and Dorte prefer their house to an apartment in the city, which would have far less space.

▼ *Dorte Fleischer outside her house. The house has lots of space for the family to keep pets.*

Every morning, Dorte drives their three children, ages two, three, and five, to kindergarten or to day care centers in the next village. Dorte and Peter are totally dependent on their cars to lead the modern village life they live.

Everybody in Hyllested knows everybody else, and the children always have somebody to visit. In that respect Hyllested is very different from the city.

"I would suffocate in a big city. I need the open spaces and fresh air. I think the village is a perfect place for my children to grow up in."
—Dorte Fleischer, teacher

▲ A fruit stand by the village roadside. Shoppers help themselves and leave the money in the bucket.

◀ Dorte Fleischer having breakfast with her children

# Denmark at Work

Most employed Danes work an average of thirty-seven hours a week, in a wide range of jobs. Denmark has a large and very important export industry, which provides thousands of jobs selling many different products all over the world. The export trade is essential to pay for all the imported products, such as clothes, electronic equipment, tropical fruits, cars, lumber, and coal.

Fishing has always been an important industry for Denmark, since it is a coastal and island country. Today, most fish are used to produce fish meal and fish oil. Farming is also very important. Danish animal products, such as bacon and ham, are well known in many countries.

▼ *Svend Bilde learned about fishing from his father. Today, an increasing number of rules and regulations make life more difficult for fishermen. All of Svend's children have found jobs in other industries.*

But most Danes are employed in service jobs, such as banking, tourism, and trade. In manufacturing, food processing is the largest sector. The production of machinery, chemical products, and electronics is also important.

Today, it is common for both men and women to have full-time jobs. Work such as building is still done mostly by men. There are also jobs, such as nursing, that are done mainly by women. However, more people every year are taking jobs that used to be done mostly by the other sex. So now, for example, there are female builders and male nurses.

Almost a third of all Danes between eighteen and sixty-six years of age are not working. They are either unemployed, being paid a pension, or have taken part-paid leave to study or to take care of their children.

| TYPES OF WORK IN DENMARK | |
|---|---|
| | **Percentage of working population** |
| **Services:** | 66% |
| **Manufacturing:** | 28% |
| **Agriculture:** | 6% |

▼ *Flight Sergeant I. M. Nielsen in the air traffic-control tower*

**"I love airplanes and I've always wanted a job in aviation. Air-traffic control is exciting. I like working with the high-tech aviation equipment."—Flight sergeant I. M. Nielsen, air-traffic controller.**

# WORK IN ÅRHUS

Every weekday morning, the roads leading into Århus are packed with cars bringing people to work. Over 35,000 people commute to the city every day, mostly by car, from villages and small towns surrounding Århus. They come to the 13,700 places of work in the city, from factories to stores and offices. There are both small and large companies, employing from one person to hundreds of people.

| TYPES OF WORK IN ÅRHUS, 1994 | |
| --- | --- |
| | Percentage of working population |
| Services: | 81% |
| Manufacturing: | 17% |
| Other: | 2% |

"I'm still at high school, but I work in a bakery on weekends to earn pocket money. Most of my friends like to earn some money, too."—Lisbeth, 18 years old

*Lisbeth at work in one of the city's many bakeries*

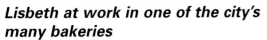

Århus Oil is a large company that produces vegetable oils, which are sold to seventy countries, including Australia and the United States. In the 1930s, Århus Oil was the biggest employer in Århus, but now only 600 people work there because machines have taken over much of the work. Since the production of vegetable oils is a high-tech process, there are sixty people working just to develop new, specialized fats and oils for dairy products, the food industry, cosmetics, and lubricants.

▲ *The offices at Århus Oil, where business with seventy countries takes place*

The harbor is an important place of work in Århus. Apart from oil and coal, more goods pass through Århus Harbor than through any other in Denmark. Containers from all over the world can be seen on the busy docks. Since the end of the Cold War, in 1989, there has been a growing number of goods that pass through the harbor on their way to Russia and the Baltic states.

▼ *A Russian tanker in Århus Harbor*

# WORK IN HYLLESTED

"I feed most of my crops to chickens, which are sold to the Middle East. Everything is mechanized. About 180,000 chickens pass through the farm every year. It's just a small farm by modern standards."—Poul Vinther, farmer (below)

Most work in Hyllested used to be in farming, but farm machinery now does many of the jobs traditionally done by hand. Today, only about a quarter of the villagers work in farming, and the farms are much bigger than they used to be.

The farms are mainly animal farms, raising pigs and cows, and most of their crops are used for animal feed. The farms produce bacon, ham, and cheese, which are sold abroad to countries such as Great Britain, Germany, the United States, and Japan.

*A combine harvester in the fields around Hyllested*

In Hyllested, there are growing numbers of small businesses that rely on modern technology and communications, such as computers and fax machines, to carry out business in the village. One business designs office furniture to be sold to Germany. There is also a small factory producing accessories for dogs, such as collars, leashes, and baskets.

*Henning Kjærgaard at the Nordtank wind-turbine factory, checking parts for a wind turbine that will be sold to India*

Other people from Hyllested work as teachers, doctors, or in other public service jobs, but mostly in nearby towns, such as Grenå. They rely on their cars to get them to work every day.

The largest factory near the village is the Nordtank wind-turbine factory, which is in the middle of farmland just outside Hyllested. Wind turbines provide an alternative source of power in Denmark, since massive public protests over twenty years ago prevented the building of nuclear power stations. This inspired companies like Nordtank to develop wind turbines for the production of electricity. Ninety percent of the turbines from Nordtank are exported to seventeen countries around the world.

# Going to School

Danish children start school when they are five or six years old. They then belong to the same class, in the same school, for the next ten years, until they are sixteen. Each class has its own class teacher, who has a close relationship with pupils and their parents. This relationship is very important in Danish schools. Sometimes classes have the same teacher for the entire ten years at school. At the age of sixteen, children take an exam before going to high school for three years, either to prepare for college or to train in a practical skill or trade.

School starts at 8:00 A.M. There are no school uniforms, and children address their teachers by their first names. Children under ten years old have four or five classes a day and finish at about 12:00 P.M., while older children have classes until about 2:00 P.M. Lunch breaks are just ten minutes long, which is just enough time to eat a sandwich brought from home. Danish schools do not have cafeterias, so all the children bring packed lunches to school.

Most younger children stay in a special day care until their parents pick them up.

*Children arriving at school by bicycle. Many children ride their bicycles to school.*

▲ *Girls grind flour the way people did in the Iron Age, in a practical history workshop. This way, they experience Iron Age living for themselves.*

Day care is important to parents because in most Danish families, both parents have full-time jobs.

It has always been considered important in Denmark for children to learn practical skills. Besides subjects like geography, math, and history, both boys and girls study woodwork, crafts, and cooking. Big school trips, called "camp school," are usually organized by the class teacher once every fourth year, with smaller trips two or three times a year. These trips are very popular with the children.

*Lunch at school* ▶ *usually consists of open sandwiches on black bread, which children bring with them from home.*

# UNIVERSITY CITY

Århus has many schools, and many young people also go to college there. Most children go to the fifty-one state schools in the city, which have up to 780 pupils each. In recent years, Århus has spent less money on schools than other large towns, which means the schools now offer slightly fewer classes and less support for children with learning difficulties. This has been particularly difficult for schools in the western parts of Århus, where the children of some immigrants speak poor Danish when they start school.

*Cooking is a popular subject in the sixth grade at Risskov School. In this picture, Kasper (below right) and Søren are preparing Danish meatballs.*

*◄ Risskov School has a very good reputation, but like many other Århus schools, it now needs money for more modern workshops to teach practical subjects such as woodwork and cooking.*

There are a number of private schools in Århus that specialize in the teaching of music, the arts, or religion. These schools have been opened by parents who want a more specialized education for their child or who are worried about the quality of education in government schools. They pay 20 percent of the costs, while the government pays the rest.

At Århus University and at the many different colleges in the city, students can study almost any subject, from history or music, to dentistry, nursing, or business studies. Århus is the only place in Denmark where students can study journalism, and the theater offers drama courses.

**"When I finish school, I want to study physiotherapy. But I may change my mind because Århus has an endless choice of courses."— Camilla Hjortshøj, 18 years old (left)**

# SCHOOL IN HYLLESTED

There have been no schools in Hyllested since 1961, when the village school was closed because there were not enough children in the village to attend it. That year, the schools in four other villages closed and a larger, central school, the Rosmus School, was built in the middle of the farmland, a mile and a quarter north of Hyllested. About 350 children go to the Rosmus School, taking a bus from several villages and farms in the area. Concentrating the children in a larger school makes it possible to have better modern equipment, such as computers, and electric guitars for music lessons.

*The fourteen children in Class 6A come from six different villages, including Hyllested.*

◀ *The school hall during a break between classes. Some children are playing games, while others are drawing or just talking.*

▼ *Rosmus School has been using computers in classrooms for many years.*

Children at the Rosmus School study the main school subjects that are taught in all Danish schools. Five times a year they can also spend one week studying a particular theme or subject. Another tradition is the annual sports day, which includes a challenging triathlon competition (a combination of swimming, running, and cycling).

Once a year, a large party is held and a school play is staged. The choir and other musical groups put on a concert every spring. Rosmus School shows that in modern Denmark, village schools are as good as city schools.

# Denmark at Play

Most Danes enjoy five weeks' vacation a year, as well as weekends, to relax and pursue their hobbies and interests. Many people join clubs to share sports or hobbies. Sports are very popular, especially soccer, gymnastics, and badminton. The two major sports associations in Denmark include over 10,000 sports clubs, with a total of 3 million members.

| DANISH PUBLIC HOLIDAYS | |
|---|---|
| New Year's Day | Jan 1 |
| Easter | March/April |
| Great Prayer Day | April/May |
| Ascension Day | May/June |
| Whit Monday | May/June |
| Constitution Day | June 5 |
| Christmas Day | December 25 |
| Boxing Day | December 26 |

*Fishing in the early spring on a canal at Sivested, central Djursland. Fishing is a popular pastime all over Denmark.*

Many Danes like to travel abroad on their vacations. In 1994, over 1.4 million vacation packages were sold in Denmark, and many other families and young people went abroad independently, so a very large percentage of the population leaves the country every year. The Mediterranean has been a popular place to go on vacation for many years. Places such as the United States, the Far East, and Australia are also becoming popular.

▲ *A family waiting to board a ferry to Anholt Island, one of the smaller Danish islands (see the map on page 5), at the start of their cycling vacation.*

Christmas is the most important holiday of the year in Denmark. Streets and stores are decorated from the middle of November, and on Christmas Eve (December 24), families gather together for a big Christmas dinner. Another Danish tradition is to walk around the Christmas tree on Christmas Eve singing carols. On Christmas Day and Boxing Day, the country nearly comes to a standstill because everybody relaxes and eats more!

▼ *A traditional Christmas Day lunch on December 25. Danish families like to celebrate Christmas and birthdays together.*

# LEISURE TIME IN ÅRHUS

"I play soccer at least three days a week. I like playing music too, but right now sports are number one."—Kasper, 12 years old

*Kasper and his twin brother, Niklas, practice soccer in a small field near their home.*

There are many ways to relax and have fun in Århus. The city has more than 500 clubs and associations, dealing with hobbies from stamp collecting to flying model aircraft.

Sports are very popular in Århus, and the city has one of the best soccer teams in Denmark, called AGF. The team is a great inspiration to young soccer players, like twelve-year-olds Kasper and Niklas, who play in one of the smaller clubs around the city.

◀ *A mock battle at the annual Viking Market in Århus*

Århus has several theaters and a very active music scene. Some of the best Danish rock bands come from Århus, and many people consider Århus to be the most lively and interesting city in Denmark, although people in Copenhagen would probably disagree!

▼ *Street performers like this one are popular during Århus Festival Week*

Århus is the home of several festivals during the year. The most famous is the annual Festival Week, in early autumn, which has a new theme every year and attracts performers and audiences from all over Denmark and abroad. Another annual festival is the Viking Market, which takes place over a long

weekend in late July, on the beach and in the forests south of Århus. At this festival, people dress, trade, work, and even fight as the Vikings used to, a thousand years ago. Mock battles have rules that make sure nobody is hurt, but they look very dramatic.

# LEISURE TIME IN HYLLESTED

Hyllested does not have the number of leisure activities that Århus has. But many are within a short drive away, in the nearby villages of Balle, Tirstrup, and Rosmus. The trip is no farther than the one that people living in the suburbs of Århus would take to reach activities in the city center.

The Hyllested Village Association organizes talks by famous people on different topics, especially on travel. The annual sports festival takes place every summer. It includes events such as aerobics, athletics, soccer, and rounders, in which both children and their parents compete. There are also various concerts by visiting orchestras in the village throughout the year. The Hyllested Hunting Association organizes talks, education, hunts, and club evenings for its members.

▼ *Children at the local music school in the village*

▼ *Children practice for the annual village rock music festival.*

*Julie and Ditte visiting their horses after school. Animals are popular with children in Hyllested, where there is more space than in Århus.*

Two scout groups that meet in Balle and Tirstrup villages are very popular with the children in Hyllested. The groups, which have both boy and girl members, learn how to sleep outdoors, cook on campfires, and build rafts. Once a year they go on a camping trip. The scouts also collect materials such as glass and paper for recycling.

Some children go to an evening class at Rosmus School, where they can choose from lots of different courses, from learning how to play a musical instrument, to doing gymnastics.

Aside from organized activities, children in Hyllested also like to entertain themselves by visiting each other after school and either watching television and listening to music or playing in their yards or in the woods nearby.

## EVENING CLASSES AT ROSMUS SCHOOL

| | |
|---|---|
| French | Basketball |
| Fashion | Accounting |
| Tractor driving | Psychology |
| Flower arranging | Hunting |
| Rock music | Fishing |
| Care of Horses | Leather crafts |
| Cooking | Motocross |

Evening classes are popular all over Denmark. They are a chance to learn something new and meet people at the same time. Classes are free for young people and charge a small fee for adults.

# The Future

Denmark has problems like every other country. There are homeless people living on the streets, and families who are frustrated by being unemployed for a long time. Some hospitals have long waiting lists, and not all old people receive the care they need. But most people in Denmark are living a life that their grandparents could only dream of. Compared with the early 1980s, Danes are spending 25 percent more on vacations, clothes, cars, furniture, and many other products.

Most people now get financial help from the government in one way or another, such as payment of their medical and dental costs, or child-support benefits.

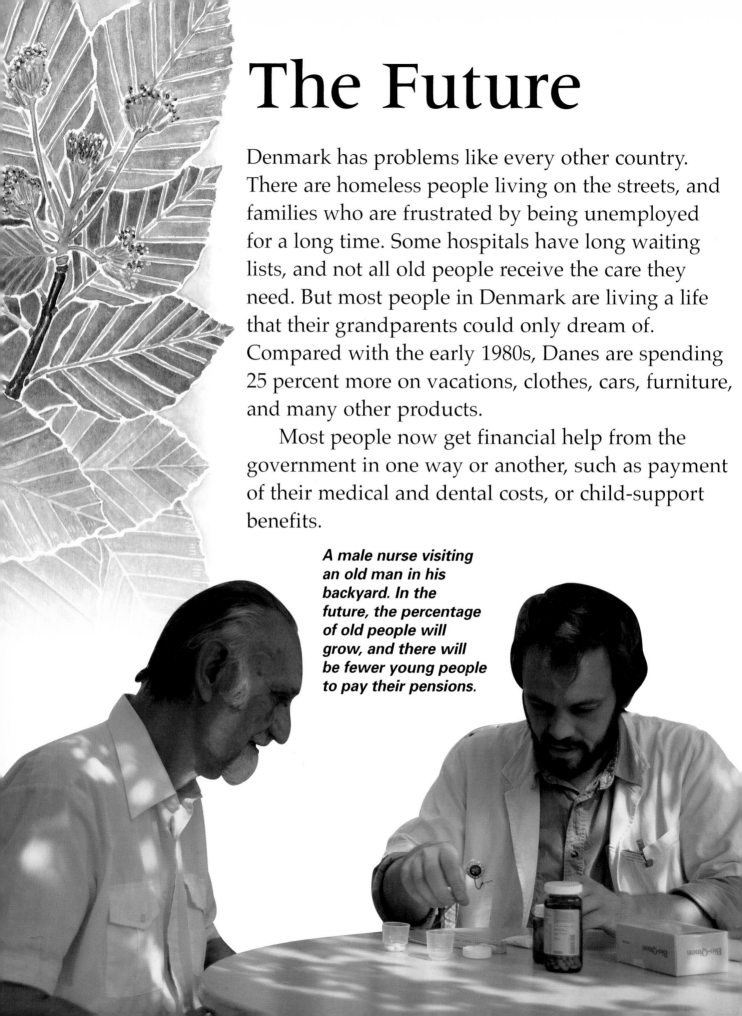

*A male nurse visiting an old man in his backyard. In the future, the percentage of old people will grow, and there will be fewer young people to pay their pensions.*

The government spends almost half its money on welfare, but some of this money is borrowed from other countries, and most people agree this cannot continue.

The big question facing Danes is how to maintain their standard of living. A Dane's hourly wage is the same as the wage for ninety hours' work in China or India. To keep this high hourly wage and standard of living, Denmark must continue to produce and sell the good ideas, designs, and products that are popular in other countries, despite their fairly high price.

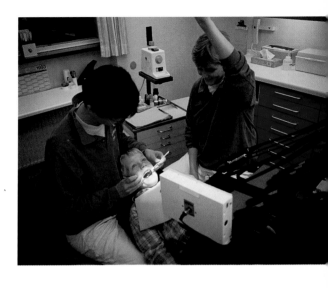

▲ *Anders Sørensen has his teeth checked at school. All children in Denmark have free dental care, which is usually provided at school.*

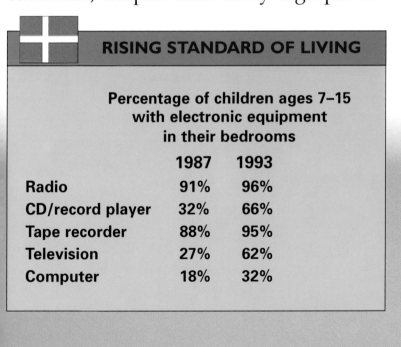

| RISING STANDARD OF LIVING | | |
| --- | --- | --- |
| Percentage of children ages 7–15 with electronic equipment in their bedrooms | | |
| | 1987 | 1993 |
| Radio | 91% | 96% |
| CD/record player | 32% | 66% |
| Tape recorder | 88% | 95% |
| Television | 27% | 62% |
| Computer | 18% | 32% |

▼ *Scandinavian Airlines (a joint Danish, Norwegian, and Swedish company) faces stiff competition from other airlines because its staff's high wages result in high fares.*

# THE FUTURE OF ÅRHUS

People in Århus are confident of a prosperous future for the city. In recent years, Århus has grown wealthier faster than the Danish average. A local newspaper that started in the city is now the country´s biggest, employing more than 1,000 people. The city has been chosen as the home of a center to develop "green" technology in Danish cities.

The Århus Music House has been a huge success. Centrally located on top of a hill near the city hall, it has helped to show the musical importance of the city. Here, people can listen to the City Symphony Orchestra, local rock and jazz bands, international superstars, or even large-scale operas.

**A children´s festival in front of the Århus Music House.**

A large amount of money was spent on the Music House. Some people thought too much was spent, but the local government stressed the importance of developing the cultural life of Århus. An active cultural life helps attract new visitors, students, and businesses.

Århus is twinned with cities in Norway and Sweden, as are many towns in Denmark, but Århus is also twinned with St. Petersburg in Russia and Harbin in China. Both are a long way from Århus, but the city is always trying to develop international links.

## ÅRHUS'S POPULATION

| | Population |
|------|------------|
| 1901 | 98,016 |
| 1960 | 221,895 |
| 1995 | 277,477 |

**Århus is continuing to grow in population as business, industry, and education attract people to the city.**

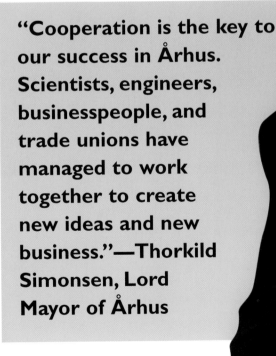

**"Cooperation is the key to our success in Århus. Scientists, engineers, businesspeople, and trade unions have managed to work together to create new ideas and new business."—Thorkild Simonsen, Lord Mayor of Århus**

# THE FUTURE OF HYLLESTED

"I expect to get even more work in the future. The months leading up to Christmas are especially busy, but there is work to be done in forests all year round."
—Peter Vinther, freelance forestry worker

There have been many changes in Hyllested over the last fifty years, and the village is still changing. Loss of population is a problem in villages all over the world. Some survive by becoming tourist attractions, which tend to make them overcrowded for part of the year and almost empty at other times. Hyllested, on the other hand, is developing new, modern businesses.

One new business is Birgitte Lyngsø's design company, which is situated in her home, in a typical, half-timbered village house. Birgitte designs children's clothes and toys. One of her latest designs is a set of medieval costumes, to be sold in Great Britain and Germany. Her clothes are tested on local children, to spot weak points or improvements that are needed. They are then made in other parts of Denmark and abroad and sold in several countries.

*Peter Vinther (left) netting Christmas trees with his Scottish friend Steven, who has come over to Denmark to work in the busy time leading up to Christmas.*

Other people in Hyllested work at home, too. There is another clothes designer and a freelance journalist in the village, and they both do business with companies in other countries.

Hyllested's survival in the future will depend on telecommunications, such as computers and fax machines, and modern transportation. They will make it possible for people in Hyllested and other villages in Denmark to continue to enjoy living and working in a village.

▲ *Birgitte Lyngsø tests two of her medieval costumes at an early stage of their design.*

## HYLLESTED'S POPULATION

|  | Population |
| --- | --- |
| 1901 | 506 |
| 1960 | 575 |
| 1995 | 430 |

**Hyllested's population has decreased since 1960, because people have moved to towns and cities for jobs.**

▼ *The arrival of more families with smaller children is a sign that Hyllested will continue to be an active village community.*

# Glossary

**Armored personnel carrier** A military vehicle usually used to transport troops in a war zone.

**Boxing Day** The first weekday after Christmas, marked by giving Christmas boxes to servants and service workers.

**Cold War** The rivalry that existed between the USSR and the United States from the end of the 1940s until the late 1980s.

**Commute** Travel between a person's home and place of work.

**Dialects** Variations in a language as it is spoken in different regions.

**European Union (EU)** A group of fifteen European countries, made up of Denmark, France, Germany, Great Britain, Italy, Ireland, Sweden, Finland, Austria, Spain, Portugal, Greece, the Netherlands, Belgium, and Luxembourg, which are working together for the interests of Europe.

**Freelance** A self-employed person, working on a temporary basis.

**"Green" technology** The development of products that do as little harm to the environment at possible.

**Half-Timbered** Made of wood framing with the spaces filled with plaster, etc.

**Ice Age** A period in history, which ended about 10,000 B.C., when the earth's climate was much colder.

**Immigrants** People who have moved from their own country to live in another country permanently.

**Iron Age** A period in history, from 500 B.C. to A.D. 700, when iron was the most important raw material for producing tools and weapons.

**Military airbase** Airfield from which military airplanes operate.

**Mock battle** A pretend battle in which the participants try to make it look realistic.

**Monarchy** A form of government headed by a sovereign, such as a king or queen.

**Peninsula** Land that is surrounded on three sides by water.

**Public service jobs** Jobs paid for by the government, such as tax collecting.

**Refugees** People who have left their own country to seek safety elsewhere.

**Rounders** A game similar to baseball played with a ball and bat.

**Suburbs** Districts on the edge of a large town or city.

**Taxes** Money paid by citizens to the government.

**Telecommunications** Communication over a distance by cable, using equipment such as telephones and faxes.

**Vacation package** A vacation that includes all the arrangements in the price.

**Welfare system** A system whereby financial help is given by the government to people who need it, such as the elderly and the unemployed.

# Further Information

## Books to Read

Garrett, Dan. *Scandinavia*. (World in View.) Austin, TX: Raintree Steck-Vaughn, 1991.

Hintz, Martin. *Denmark*. (Enchantment of the World.) Danbury, CT: Children's Press, 1994.

Lerner Geography Staff, ed. *Denmark in Pictures*. (Visual Geography.) Minneapolis, MN: Lerner Group, 1991.

McLeish, Ewan. *Europe*. (Continents.) Austin, TX: Raintree Steck-Vaughn, 1997.

## Useful Address

Danish Embassy
32 Whitehaven Street
Washington, DC 20008
(202) 234-4300

## Picture acknowledgments

All photographs except page 25 (top) are by Ole Steen Hansen. Page 25 (top): Århus Oil.
All maps are by Hardlines.
Border artwork is by Kate Davenport.

# Index

Page numbers in **bold** refer to photographs.